Discover Cats

by Katrina Streza

© 2017 by Katrina Streza
ISBN: 978-1-53240-270-4
eISBN: 978-1-53240-2081
Images licensed from Fotolia.com
All rights reserved.
No portion of this book may be reproduced
without express permission of the publisher.
First Edition
Published in the United States by
Xist Publishing
www.xistpublishing.com
PO Box 61593 Irvine, CA 92602

There are many different kinds, or breeds of cats.

Some cats have long, thick fur and some cats have no fur at all.

Cats can be different colors. The colors help us know the cat breed.

When cats are born, their eyes are dark blue. When they grow up, their eyes change to yellow, green, gold, or light blue.

Baby cats are called kittens.
This little kitten is alone.

Kittens do not like to be alone. This little kitten looks in the mirror for a friend.

The kittens found friends. Some cats are sad if they have no friends.

When this cat wants to play, he wiggles his tail.

These two kittens see something up high. What do they see?

19

They see a toy! Cats love to play with toys.

If a cat sees a toy, it will jump to try to catch the toy. Cats can jump eight feet!

When cats are tired, they yawn or roll on the ground. Cats can sleep anywhere.

Kittens need to eat food to grow strong. This kitten will eat dry cat food.

Some cats try to eat mice.
This cat looks at a mouse.

If cats eat too much, they get fat. This cat is too fat to jump.

Some cats can learn to do tricks. This cat is waving "goodbye!"

www.ingramcontent.com/pod-product-compliance
Lightning Source LLC
LaVergne TN
LVHW010020070426
835507LV00001B/19